SHARKS
AN IMAGINATION LIBRARY SERIES

SHARK CAMOUFLAGE AND ARMOR

by Victor Gentle and Janet Perry

Gareth Stevens Publishing
A WORLD ALMANAC EDUCATION GROUP COMPANY

Please visit our web site at: www.garethstevens.com
For a free color catalog describing Gareth Stevens' list of high-quality books and
multimedia programs, call 1-800-542-2595 (USA) or 1-800-461-9120 (Canada).
Gareth Stevens Publishing's Fax: (414) 332-3567.

Library of Congress Cataloging-in-Publication Data

Gentle, Victor.
    Shark camouflage and armor / by Victor Gentle and Janet Perry.
       p. cm. — (Sharks: an imagination library series)
    Includes bibliographical references and index.
    ISBN 0-8368-2827-5 (lib. bdg.)
    1. Sharks—Morphology—Juvenile literature. 2. Animal defenses—Juvenile literature.
    3. Camouflage (Biology)—Juvenile literature. [1. Sharks. 2. Camouflage (Biology).
    3. Animal defenses.] I. Perry, Janet, 1960- II. Title.
    QL638.9.G3588   2001
    597.3'147—dc21   00-052247

First published in 2001 by
Gareth Stevens Publishing
A World Almanac Education Group Company
330 West Olive Street, Suite 100
Milwaukee, WI 53212 USA

Text: Victor Gentle and Janet Perry
Page layout: Victor Gentle, Janet Perry, and Scott Krall
Cover design: Scott Krall
Series editor: Heidi Sjostrom
Picture Researcher: Diane Laska-Swanke

Photo credits: Cover, pp. 5 (inset), 13 © Doug Perrine/Innerspace Visions; p. 5 (main)
© Franco Banfi/Innerspace Visions; p. 7 © James D. Watt/Innerspace Visions; pp. 9, 15 (both)
© Mark Conlin/Innerspace Visions; p. 11 (both) © Scott W. Michael/Innerspace Visions;
p. 17 © Rudie Kuiter/Innerspace Visions; p. 19 © Tsuneo Nakamura/Innerspace Visions;
p. 21 © Nigel Marsh/Innerspace Visions

Printed in the United States of America

1 2 3 4 5 6 7 8 9 05 04 03 02 01

Front cover: This nurse shark takes a nap next to a large coral fan. The shark
is well protected by the way the color of its skin blends with the ocean floor.
Notice the way its **denticles** glitter in the light from the water's surface.

TABLE OF CONTENTS

Words that appear in the glossary are printed in **boldface** type the first time they occur in the text.

SNEAK ATTACK

Sharks protect themselves with their own **camouflage** and **armor**. Besides mouths full of teeth and powerful bodies, they have spots and stripes on their bodies so they can hide to catch food or trick other animals into staying away from them. Sharks also have spines and teeth on their skin. All this is just to catch their food and to avoid being eaten.

There are two kinds of camouflage for sharks. One kind allows the shark to hide because it looks so similar to its surroundings. Another allows the shark to confuse other animals into thinking it is not a shark, but a bigger fish.

See how the water shadows on the Galapagos shark in the small picture are similar to the skin patterns that look like water shadows on the horn shark in the larger picture?

HIDE AND SEEK!

Most sharks have some sort of coloring that helps them blend in with their surroundings.

Even sharks that live in the open ocean are colored in a way that protects them from being noticed. The upper (**dorsal**) halves of their bodies, near the surface of the ocean, are darker than the lower (**ventral**) halves. The dorsal side might be a dark shade of gray, blue, or brown. The ventral side would be a much lighter shade of gray, blue, or brown. This is called **countershading**.

Because of countershading, it's easier for these sharks to sneak up and catch their food. Countershading might also help them escape notice by humans, who are their most common **predators**.

Even though this blue shark hunts in the open ocean, where there is no place for it to hide, its coloring makes it hard to see in the waters where it swims.

I'M STILL HIDING!

Have you ever wished you could hide right out in the open, just by being as still as a rock?

Angel sharks do just that. Their skin color is almost the same as the color of the ocean's sandy floor. This camouflage makes it very difficult to see angel sharks — especially when they flip sand on their backs with their front fins.

Because of the angel shark's coloring, predators (the animals that like to eat angel sharks) might swim right past. Or the animals that angel sharks like to eat (their **prey**) might get close enough to be munched up — without ever knowing what happened!

Angel sharks live on the ocean floor near shorelines where divers often mistake them for sand and step on them. Divers call angel sharks and other flat sharks dangerous, but the sharks are just protecting themselves.

KIDDIE CAMOUFLAGE

Young sharks are usually left on their own as soon as they are born. One way that many young sharks defend themselves is to have patterns on their skin that trick predators. These patterns make it easy for young sharks to hide in caves, under seaweed, and in **coral forests** until they grow up. Their parents don't protect them, but their coloring does.

The brown-banded bamboo shark is a small shark during its whole life. It needs to hide from bigger fish when it's out hunting for food. It doesn't have just one camouflage suit, though. It has two! This shark is striped and spotted when it's young, but it is a light brown color all over when it's an adult. Either way, it hides really well in its surroundings.

The small picture shows a baby brown-banded bamboo shark with all its baby stripes. The large picture shows the adult shark, with a brown color that hides it well along rocky shores.

WHAT BIG EYES YOU HAVE!

The **epaulette** shark has two ways of tricking predators. Its body is covered with spots and colors that blend with its surroundings. But it also has special markings that can fool a predator into believing that the epaulette shark is bigger than it really is.

The large spot on the epaulette, just behind the gills, is shaped just like the eye of a larger fish. Predators might stay away from the epaulette shark because they see it as being too big for them to catch and eat.

Which eyes are the ones that see? See how the large spot just above this shark's front fin has a circle of white around it? To other fish, the spot looks like the eye of a MUCH bigger fish.

SMALL, SWELL SHARK

Like the epaulette shark, the swell shark has two ways to trick predators. First, the swell shark has camouflage markings that allow it to hide in the rocks and shallow water weeds. Second, it can suck in water to make itself seem to be a larger fish than it is.

If a predator still decides that a swell shark is just the right size for a meal, the swell shark has one more way to escape being dinner. It uses its swelling power to wedge itself so strongly into the cracks between some rocks that no predator can pull it out.

In the small picture, the swell shark might look small and easy to munch up. In the large picture, you can see how it swells up to twice its usual size when it sucks in water!

POINTED PROTECTION

Many sharks are sharp all over. They have spines in front of their dorsal fins and teeth inside and out.

The "teeth" on shark skin are called **denticles.** Scientists think the denticles and spines have two purposes. First, they make it hard for predators to swallow a shark whole, or even to get just a bite.

Second, all that pointy stuff might make sharks faster swimmers. The denticles are shaped so that water flows smoothly over the shark's body. The water doesn't drag on the shark and slow it down.

Some sharks also have a **nictitating membrane**, a third eyelid that protects their eyes from attacks — by either fierce predators or by prey that fights back.

This prickly dogfish sparkles under bright lights. But don't pet the pretty shark! All those glittery things are "teeth," and just look at the spikes next to its fins!

SHARK ARSENALS

Some sharks have their own very special weapons to defend themselves. One of these sharks is the saw shark. It has a very long snout with teeth on it, like a saw. When a saw shark is attacked, it slashes its "saw" at the enemy.

The saw shark also uses its "saw" to hunt food. If it chases a swimming animal, the saw shark might use its saw to hit and stun the fish. Then it is easy for the saw shark to catch and eat the fish.

If the saw shark is digging around for food on the ocean floor, it will churn up the sand and then whack at its prey until the prey is confused and hurt so badly that it can't move. Then, the saw shark gobbles it up.

In addition to all the teeth on its snout, this saw shark has **barbels** dangling from its "saw." These barbels sense pulses and chemicals in the water, helping the saw shark find food.

EQUIPPED FOR DANGER

It may seem strange that sharks need so many ways to protect themselves from attacks. After all, a large number of people think that sharks are some of the most dangerous animals on the planet.

However, young baby sharks take a long time to grow to their adult size. So they need extra protection just to grow up. Also, most sharks are rather small as adults, well under 5 feet (1.5 meters) long. They are often prey for larger sharks. And sharks can even be attacked back by their own food!

Even so, it's no wonder that sharks, big and small, have survived 400 million years. Glittering denticles have shielded their bodies from harm. And beautiful patterns and clever colors have hidden them.

The wobbegong looks like a pretty rug on the ocean floor. But don't wipe your feet on it! This rug bites back if it's stomped upon.

MORE TO READ AND VIEW

Books (Nonfiction)   *Marine Biologist: Swimming with the Sharks. Risky Business* (series)
        Keith Greenberg, Tim Calver, Bruce Glassman, and Doug Perrine
        (Blackbirch Press)
    Sharks (series). Victor Gentle and Janet Perry (Gareth Stevens)
    Watch Out for Sharks. Caroline Arnold and Richard Hewitt
        (Houghton Mifflin)

Books (Activity)   *A Look Inside Sharks and Rays.* Keith Banister (Reader's Digest)
    Tropical Fish. Neal Pronek (Chelsea House Publishing)
    Whales, Sharks and Other Sea Creatures. Draw Science (series)
        Nina Kidd (Lowell House Juvenile)

Books (Fiction)   *Shark Beneath the Reef.* Jean Craighead George (HarperCollins)
    Sharks!: True Stories and Legends. Catherine Gourley (Millbrook Press)
    'Ula Li'i and the Magic Shark. Donivee Martin Laird (Barnaby Books)

Videos (Nonfiction)   *Great White Shark.* (20th Century Fox)
    *National Geographic's Really Wild Animals: Secret Weapons and Great
        Escapes.* (National Geographic)

PLACES TO WRITE AND VISIT

Here are three places to contact for more information:

Greenpeace
702 H Street NW
Washington, DC 20001
USA
1-202-462-1177
www.greenpeace.org

World Wildlife Fund
1250 24th Street NW, Suite 500
Washington, DC 20037
USA
1-800-CALL-WWF
www.wwf.org

Vancouver Aquarium
P.O. Box 3232
Vancouver, BC
Canada V6B 3X8
1-604-659-3474

To find a zoo or aquarium to visit, check out **www.aza.org** and, on the American Zoo and Aquarium's home page, look under <u>AZA Services</u>, and click on <u>Find a Zoo or Aquarium</u>.

WEB SITES

If you have your own computer and Internet access, great! If not, most libraries have Internet access. The Internet changes every day, and web sites come and go. We believe the sites we recommend here are likely to last, and that they give the best and most appropriate links for our readers to pursue their interest in sharks and their environment.

www.ajkids.com

This is the junior Ask Jeeves site — it's a great research tool. Some questions to try out in Ask Jeeves Kids:

> *What shapes are sharks' denticles?*
> *What are sharks' spines for?*

You can also just type in words and phrases with "?" at the end, for example:

> *Wobbegongs?*
> *Swell sharks?*

www.mbayaq.org/lc/kids_place/kidseq.asp

This is the Kids' E-quarium of the Monterey Bay Aquarium. Make postcards, print out coloring pages, play games, go on a virtual deep-sea dive, or find out about some marine science careers.

oberon.educ.sfu.ca/splash/tank.htm

It's the Touch Tank. Click on a critter or a rock in the aquarium to see more about it.

www.pbs.org/wgbh/nova/sharks/world/clickable.html

It's the Clickable Shark. Click on any part of the shark picture to find out how sharks work.

www2.orbit.net.mt/sharkman/index.htm

Enter the Sharkman's World near Malta. He's a scuba diver who is completely soaked in anything even a little bit sharky. You'll find poetry, music, and shark pictures there. The Sharkman is not a scientist, but he loves to talk sharks with other shark fans — like you!

kids.discovery.com/KIDS

Click on the Live SharkCam. See a live leopard shark and live blacktip reef sharks!

www.pbs.org/wgbh/nova/sharks/world/whoswho.html

Here's a shark "family tree." Click on any of the titles, and you'll see what kinds of sharks belong in the same group, and why. If you see a picture of a shark you don't know, use the Shark-O-Matic to get answers.

SharkCove.homestead.com/index.html

This is Shark Girl's page! This is a creative, informative, lively, and "100% kid safe" page created by an enthusiastic shark lover. Good graphics, amusing and educational sections, and good links are featured.

GLOSSARY

You can find these words on the pages listed. Reading a word in a sentence helps you understand it even better.

armor (AR-mur) — a hard covering that protects from injury 4, 16

barbels (BAR-belz) — fleshy sense organs that sense movements and smells and hang near or on the snouts of sharks and other fish 18

camouflage (KAM-oh-flahj) — coloring that blends with the background so that animals can hide easily or confuse others 4, 8, 10, 14

coral forests (KOR-ul FOR-ests) — large groups of coral that look like large groups of trees 10

countershading (KOWN-ter-SHAY-ding) — when a shark or other animal has a darker color is on the top side of its body and a lighter color on the underside 6

denticles (DEN-ti-kulz) — tiny toothlike plates that cover a shark's skin 2, 16, 20

dorsal (DOR-sul) — on the top side or backbone, such as a dorsal fin 6, 16

epaulette (eh-puh-LET) — a braid-trimmed decoration, usually on the shoulder of a military uniform. Epaulette sharks are called that because of the white edge outlining their fins 12, 14

nictitating membrane (NIK-ti-TAY-ting MEM-brain) — a third eyelid that protects some sharks from injury to their eyes 16

predators (PREH-duh-torz) — animals that hunt prey animals for food 6, 8, 10, 12, 14, 16

prey (PRAY) — the animals hunted for food by predators 8, 16, 18, 20

ventral (VEN-trull) — on the underside or belly of animals or plants 6

INDEX